THE CULTS

How to Respond
Updated Edition

Hubert F. Beck

A CHRISTIAN WITNESS

CONCORDIA PUBLISHING HOUSE · SAINT LOUIS

This edition published 2010 Concordia Publishing House.
Text copyright © 1977, 1995 Concordia Publishing House.
3558 S. Jefferson Avenue, St. Louis, MO 63118–3968

1-800-325-3040 • www.cph.org

Originally published as *How to Respond to the Cults* in The Response Series © 1977 Concordia Publishing House.

Manufactured in the United States of America

Library of Congress Cataloging-in-Publication Data

Beck, Hubert F.
The cults / Hubert F. Beck.—Rev. ed.
    Satanism / Bruce G. Frederickson.
        p.   cm.   — (How to respond series)
    Rev. ed. of: How to respond to ... the cults. © 1977.
    Includes bibliographical references.

    ISBN 0–7586-1621-X
    1. Cults—United States—Controversial literature.   2. Christian sects—United States—Controversial literature. 3. United States—Church history—20th century. . I. Beck, Hubert F. How to respond to—the cults. II. Title. III. Series.
    BL2525.B4215 1995
    200'.973—dc20   95–10751

1 2 3 4 5 6 7 8 9 10   19 18 17 16 15 14 13 12 11 10

CONTENTS

1 CHARACTERISTICS OF CULTS

DEFINITIONS

The difficulty in defining a "cult" can be illustrated by a sampling of definitions:

"A cult is a religious perversion," says Dave Breese. "It is a belief and practice in the world of religion which calls for devotion to a religious view or leader centered in false doctrine. It is an organized heresy."[1]

Ronald Enroth quotes Margaret Singer, who stated that the word cult itself "has been variously applied to groups involved in beliefs and practices just off the beat of traditional religions; to groups making exploratory excursions into non-Western philosophical practices; and to groups involving intense relationships between followers and a powerful idea or leader."[2]

Dr. Walter Martin emphasizes the importance of a central figure to a cult. He says that "a cult might also be defined as a group of people gathered about a specific person or person's misinterpretation of the Bible."[3]

Broad definitions are necessary when defining a cult.[4] Cults clearly offer religious options that vary significantly from those expressions with which people are normally acquainted. Yet it is sometimes difficult to determine just when a group is or has become a cult.

The cult often begins as a fringe group to an accepted religion. Then, under the influence of a strong central figure, it moves away from its original roots and takes on a life of its own. Its teachings always vary considerably from those of its parent body and often are a twisted distortion.

Cultic deviations can come from any religious grouping, not just Christianity. Cults exist in virtually all world religions. Baha'is and Black Muslims are cultic deviations from Islam. The Hare Krishna religion is an altered form of Hinduism.

Cults, then, are not merely marginal statements of their original religious patterns. They totally depart from the religious thought out of which they sprang. Their way of speaking may sound familiar, and a person might recognize some parts of their religious roots. Yet they warp and twist their expression of those roots so that the original intentions are no longer present. Something altogether different has come forth.

CULTS—THE UNPAID BILLS OF THE CHURCH

Cultic language springs from the orthodox language of its parenting body. That is one reason they confuse Christians so easily. Cults use language recognizable, at least in part, by people rooted in major religious systems. It is difficult to sort through what they brought *from* the orthodox parenting body and what has been manipulated and twisted *out* of its original intentions. Orthodox words and thoughts are constantly given new and different understandings. A confusing sort of double-talk has evolved.

Examples abound. Jehovah's Witnesses speak of "everlasting death," by which they mean "annihilation," a denial of the resurrection of all flesh. They speak reverently of Jesus as "a created individual; a god," thereby denying Jesus' coequality with the Father and the Holy Spirit. Normal dialogue, filled with such alterations of meanings, is almost impossible.

Those twisting the terms can sound so persuasive. They are very knowledgeable, both about the orthodox understandings *against* which they speak and the new way they have of presenting those understandings. They present their case as though there were no other explanation. This very confidence makes them sound absolutely convincing.

Although the job is difficult, Christians need to engage members of these cults in dialogue. On the one hand, we need to challenge their definition and use of terms. On the other hand, we need to witness to the full force such terms have in their historic usage in the Church. The cults' perversions of the timeless truths of God challenge the Church to be faithful in presenting its message to the world more clearly and aggressively. When we do so, cult members are called to respond to the actual message and mission of the Church. Because we have not always done our job, one author has called the cults "the unpaid bills of the church."[4]

> "In your hearts honor Christ the Lord as holy, always being prepared to make a defense to anyone who asks you for a reason for the hope that is in you; yet do it with gentleness and respect" (1 Peter 3:15).

THE MENTALITY OF THE CULTS

8

There is, then, no one umbrella under which all cults may be placed, and we must avoid overgeneralization. Yet some marks of the cults are common enough that a "mentality of the cults" can be identified. ✳

The doctrine of the last days and last things is a frequent theme among cults. Cults emphasize signs pointing to the imminent end of the world in their teachings. For example, the "thousand-year reign" of Jehovah following the great battle of Armageddon is stressed among groups such as Jehovah's Witnesses and the Seventh-day Adventists. Signs and warnings of how rapidly the world is falling into judgment take on a flavor and intention all their own in the cults.

Prophecy and fulfillment themes also reveal the mentality of the cults. Quoting selected prophecies and coupling them with selected "fulfillments" in world events often exerts tremendous influence on people. This use of Scripture is highly selective and very manipulative.

Special revelations (often specifically to the cultic leader) frequently form the basis for "correct" interpretation of a particular prophecy and its fulfillment. This, of course, makes dialogue with such groups extremely difficult. How can one reasonably disagree when special revelations have been given from God to a particular person? There is no space for reason. All discussion is based on the leader's authority, which, in turn, is based on special revelation alone.

The authority of the cult leader is regularly exercised in the interpretation of the "inner secrets," meaning "saving knowledge." Revelations, secret rituals, and symbols require authoritarian interpretation. Only those "on the inside" can have this authority. This sense of secretiveness also gives rise to castes or inner structures of authority to preserve and pass on this "inside knowledge." The Mormon Church exemplifies such authoritarian practice.

Most cults are very dogmatic. They do not tolerate deviations from their teachings and life. Some cults, such as that of the Baha'i or cults grounded in Eastern religions, may appear tolerant, but this surface often disappears as a person moves to the heart of their teachings and practice.

A form of double-talk also characterizes cults. By this, we mean that they use ordinary terms in special ways that only the cult members understand. Since this special use of terms varies considerably from cult to cult, there is no way to be certain that one understands a second cult when one has "mastered" the vocabulary of the first one. The one thing that *must* be kept in mind is this: What a word means to you is not what it may mean to a cult member. This makes dialogue with cult members difficult.

A complete lack of interest in logical consistency accompanies this double-talk. The mental flip-flops that members of cults make bewilder the ordinary hearer. Their greatest inconsistencies, in fact, often occur at precisely the most crucial junctures, causing great difficulty in carrying on ordinary conversations. Drawing their attention to this only makes them certain that the listener has not yet seen the light.

Cults are convinced that *their "way" will be proved in the end.* Some groups, of course, have no particular anticipations of victory. Those involved in transcendental meditation, for example, would not speak of an "end" or "proof" or "victory." Yet ultimate authentication in some great and final sign is a common characteristic of most cults.

Warnings of the world's end; prophecy and fulfillment; high authority; inner secrets; intense dogmatism; little tolerance; special revelations; double-talk; lack of inner consistency; lack of a sense of sin; a different view of salvation; highly compartmentalized lives; messianic ideas—all are part of a cultic mentality.

The concept of sin is frequently minimized or totally absent in the language of the cults. When spoken of, "sin" is equated with resisting or living outside the boundaries of their teachings and/or lifestyles. *Inside* their ranks, though, they clearly teach and live according to a "right way." Therefore, sin is not commonly spoken of in their midst since they know and live "the way."

Minimizing sin affects what the cults mean when using words like *salvation*. "To be saved" has little to do with a right relationship with God; it means membership and participation in the cult itself. This quite typically places the authoritative leader into a "messianic" or "saving" office for the cult—whether that claim was originally made or not.

Cults also insist on a highly disciplined framework of thought and life. Nonmembers commonly feel quite challenged—often intimidated or shamed—by the intense discipline and commitment of cult members. Theirs is a total way of life followed with absolute strictness.

This leads to *a highly segregated life.* In many cases, members have little or no serious contact with the outside world. Their beliefs have removed them from the world that most people experience. They do feel "sent" into the world to snatch the unenlightened out of the world, yet they seldom enter the world as learners or participants. And when they do, cult members sound like taped versions of one another. They have been taught formulized understandings and responses to almost anything and everything.

Cult members feel "freed" from "religious exploitation" simply because of their membership in the cult. This bewilders the "outsider," because cult members appear both imprisoned and exploited by the cult. Here one sees what a mind-job is done by cultic leaders. They impress upon followers that liberation from all outside religious oppression takes place only within the cult. Only in the cult can a person be dedicated to the most full and free expression of life.

Rarely, if ever, would all of the above be found in one cult, but many of them will appear quite consistently. When several of them are in a single group, one can almost certainly identify the group as a cult.

A final caution: Because cults usually include at least one unusual but visible teaching, nonmembers often think of that one item as the main difference between the cult and its parent group. However, that item often is a non-essential or a relatively minor matter. For example, when people think of Jehovah's Witnesses, blood transfusions and a refusal to pledge allegiance to the flag usually come to mind. Focusing on such surface items is deceptive since the points of division lie much deeper than that and are more serious.

2 WHY THE SURGE OF CULTS IN OUR DAY?

CULTURAL FACTORS

A Disenchantment with Intellect

In recent decades, an anti-intellectual trend has arisen. Since technological advances change so quickly, any hope for a bright future has been largely dashed. Many feel that intellectual answers to the world's problems have created more problems than they have solved. Therefore, many people give new ways of dealing with life serious consideration.

One reaction has been to place a greater emphasis on the unseen rather than on what can be analyzed. And since we have authority over our feelings, how we feel has become more important than what we think.

With this new focus on feelings, it has become important to look inside one's self in order to find out what happens there and to understand life better. Thinking generally requires looking outside one's self to determine the factors that affect a person in life. If you look inside yourself, you are beyond anyone's control. Others may control your external life, but nobody can control your inner life.

Getting in touch with your feelings, then, enables you to discover who you are. Ultimately this means that *feeling well* takes precedence over *being well.* This mood pervades our day in many circles. Cults promise "good feelings" to people tired of "feeling bad" by the way "thinking people" manipulate and control them. So the person who wants to feel good finds it easy to join a cult.

THE MOOD OF RELATIVITY

A conviction that "nothing is sure; everything is relative" permeates today's world. This sense of uncertainty comes partially through science. New research regularly uncovers information that seems to contradict old and formerly indisputable facts. If even such sure things as scientific facts constantly

Cults promise to make people "feel good about themselves." Since intellect has failed to bring about a bright new world where people are happy, why not try the cults?

16

change, why shouldn't all knowledge be subject to change?

The above-mentioned shift from logical thought to feeling adds to the idea that everything is relative. It even permeates religion. Because "revealed truth" varies from culture to culture, no single culture can claim an absolute truth (so the thinking goes). After all, doesn't a person "feel" religion more than "think" it? And doesn't the same logic lead one to say that what "feels right" will actually "be right"? Therefore, strong influences reinforce the mood of relativity that pervades our age.

When there is such a lack of surety in life, insecurity sets in. We seem to be floating on a sea of uncertainty. Society seems to give no sense of direction. There is no guide into a secure tomorrow. When a sense of insecurity becomes too great for a person to bear, that person starts looking for something to be sure of. When cults present beliefs and a way of life grounded in "certainty," they become very attractive in this setting. Even if that "certainty" is a bit weird or different at first, so what? Everything about our age seems strange and different from previous ages. Emerging new religious forms are just part of a newly emerging world, are they not? How easily people can be victimized in this setting of relativity!

THE NEED FOR HUMAN COMMUNITY

A person needs to feel wanted. Loneliness is one of the most pervasive feelings now. Our society greatly stresses the individual; you must be "your own person." The cost has been immense. We have lost a sound sense of community.

Loneliness is as old as Adam and Eve. Their sin separated them immediately, not only from God but also from each other. They became adversaries rather than friends. Sin pitted Cain against Abel. Sin isolates people, and isolation ruptures the human community. People are cut off from one another. Yet we all have an intense drive toward human community. Therefore, humans have devised many ways of living meaningfully with one another in life together.

Societies have generally organized themselves around tribes and villages. Even cities had smaller subsets within which people knew one another quite well. These settings made it clear that everyone's mutual good depended on the welfare of the society they shared.

It has become more difficult in recent years, however, to arrange life around intimate relationships. A fragmented life prevents us from knowing very many people deeply and intimately. We meet and relate casually to many different people, but we do not easily find friendships that run deep. And those that do are hard to maintain.

Today's high mobility is a part of this. Since we know that a friendship made today may well be broken tomorrow, we keep relationships looser, less intense, in order to risk less grief and sorrow if a separation does occur.

Furthermore, consider the sense of fulfillment that comes from living a ruggedly individualistic life. People admire the self-made person, so we want to become such a person. If we are not self-sufficient, we are a nobody. We are also told to have friends we can run and party with but not to depend on them. Do not make community with them. Besides, "if you don't look out for yourself, nobody else will." Words like this warn us to distrust others. In such a climate, how can any sense of community survive and thrive?

Yet we long to belong. We yearn to be a member of a caring community where wounds are bandaged and happiness can be shared. The cults' promise of such an enticing place of intimate closeness and caring draws people in like a magnet.

American stress on individualism has created a nation of lonely people. The cults, presenting a promise of close, familial ties, take advantage of this loneliness.

Again the phrase echoes in our ears: "The cults are the unpaid bills of the church." The Church is meant to be a community, the fellowship of the Body of Christ. The whole New Testament sets forth this vision. But too many lonely people do not find in the Church a place that heals their loneliness. So a cult becomes the next best thing.

THE RISE IN LEISURE TIME

Strangely enough, even though we have more leisure time than ever before, most people claim to be busier than ever. We have filled time once spent on surviving with time spent on leisure. Instead of planting, sowing, and harvesting, we cart children to dance lessons, we play golf, and we buy go to fitness clubs. We keep busy, but not with what we need to survive.

Compared to a hundred or two hundred years ago, we have a lot more leisure time. But unless we fill our free time, we feel a loss of purpose. In the midst of such a void, people tend to ask, "What is life all about?" Significantly, people today are asking the same question even while occupied with their new leisure time busyness.

Then, question of meaning easily gives way to another question: "Am I *really* happy?" And we passionately begin seeking happiness to fill our emptiness.

This stress on feelings takes its toll. Many people find themselves unsatisfied with life. Being surrounded by abundance and affluence does not necessarily fulfill life and often becomes downright boring. To have everything yet still want more becomes frustrating, especially when added to an inability to find meaning in what we have and do. We passionately hope *someone* will help us find that for which we so desperately long.

Cults have found a way to use this passion for happiness and self-fulfillment. They know the value of someone who is strongly committed to a cause in order to gain a sense of significance and a sense of being needed. Happiness lies in this direction rather than in the direction of comfort and wealth.

"The cults are the unpaid bills of the church." The echo haunts us. Jesus lays the divine cause before us and offers opportunities for a life of meaningful service in His kingdom. Where the Church has failed in today's world to communicate the cause of Christ and His call to commitment, the cults have moved into the void to fill it.

THE AUTHORITY—FREEDOM STRUGGLE

The need for authority and the drive for freedom also becomes part of the mix. How can we remain free and yet subject enough to authority to maintain order within the world? Are we even agreed on what the terms mean? Some people understand *freedom* as license to do whatever one pleases. Thus defined, it removes all restraint and gives full sway to the rule of one's feelings. "If you feel like it, do it!"

"Does life have any real meaning?" is a major question of our day. Cults use this question to their advantage.

However, there is a vast difference between "freedom" and "license." Freedom maintains responsibility while choosing from a number of options. It restrains itself when necessary. It seeks the common good. Freely giving up one's rights in the interest of others does not infringe on personal rights. Given that understanding of freedom, "what I feel like doing" will never become an excuse to be unscrupulous.

Authority must be exercised with the same restraint for the common good. It is not merely a form of personal advantage. Used properly, authority becomes a form of service as it arranges life with the good of others in mind.

Thus, neither authority nor freedom are absolute. They are held in tension, and both become meaningful within that tension.

So where, how, and by whom is authority wielded? May it ever be resisted? Who says what is right or wrong? These are important questions of our day. Note what's happening. Children reprimanded for pre-marital sex see adults modeling promiscuity. Politicians are notorious for having double standards. Those who ask others to keep their laws do not abide by their own regulations; why should you? Why not become a law unto yourself? Do what you feel like doing; everyone else is.

Many raise the same questions about religious authority. Since faith is a private and individual matter (nobody can believe for us), it is asserted that no one should tell us what to believe. However, a faith reduced to this extinguishes the truth. If truth is whatever you want it to be, it can never be objectively identified. Nor can it be communicated. Therefore, every person and generation must discover its own truth. Whatever you "feel" becomes right and true. Religious authority becomes meaningless, or so it is claimed.

However, real truth has substance to it. The historical experience of the ages affirms the existence of truth.

Religious authority reflects on this substance called truth that has sustained the ages. It needs interpreters and teachers to move it from age to age, from culture to culture. And it needs God's revelation, for we need the facts that are true apart from our human subjective opinion and condition.

Cults manipulate this need by offering people a "definitive word" apart from that which has long been known. People left to believe what they want become confused and bewildered. Cults move into this vacuum. They convince new recruits that there is not only something definite but also new to know and by which to live.

Once more the phrase haunts us: "The cults are the unpaid bills of the church." The proper tension between authority and freedom has been hard to determine in the modern world. Cults have prospered because the question of who possesses and correctly interprets the truth that makes us free is neglected in our world today. The Church has also failed to deal with that question wisely or well.

RELIGIOUS FACTORS

The meaning of the phrase "the cults are the unpaid bills of the church" can be seen in light of the preceding cultural factors. It becomes even clearer when several important religious factors are also put into the picture.

Shallow Religious Understandings

A notable lack of biblical knowledge exists among members of churches in our day. While our nation has never been the uniquely "Christian nation" so many suggest, there has been a biblical undercurrent running through our public life throughout our history. Even non-Christians have been influenced (sometimes more than they care to admit).

That biblical awareness, however, has been largely watered down and lost. Compared to our ancestors, Christians as well as non-Christians today have, at best, a superficial knowledge of Scripture. Members of churches with longer periods of instruction for children have retained some of the biblical content and message. Even among them, though, one rarely finds well-informed adults able to converse in the language of the Bible or the Christian faith.

Poorly informed Christians are not only ineffective but often injured in any dialogue with well-informed and committed cult members. If all we know about Scripture and Christianity comes from our childhood, we will not

25

stand up against such an assault. The only thing poorly informed people can do is to cave in or hide.

Obviously, we need to know more than merely additional biblical content. We also need to know how to use the Bible, how to show the way its parts fit and work together in presenting God's truth. We need to know how to do this because the cults regularly *mis*use passages from the Bible. Without instruction in how to use Scripture, Christians will be easy prey for the cults.

THE MEANING OF LIFE

The question raised earlier about the meaning of life returns to the picture as a religious question. On the one hand, the Bible offers a simple response in terms of loving God and our neighbor. On the other hand, the Bible reflects a deep awareness of this complicated question.

> Better grasp of the Bible's contents, as well as how to use it, is imperative if Christians are ever to meaningfully confront the cults.

This fundamental inquiry is answered in many ways. Some seek meaning in life in how they deal with suffering and trouble. Others seek it in the acquisition of possessions. Still others seek it in relationships. Most people recognize that the answer does not lie in the material world but in the spiritual. Yet despite the many answers available, despair still abounds. For some people, all answers ring hollow.

The Church responds to the question by proclaiming the Gospel of Christ. But that message, too, has become garbled. Some church leaders debate which of Jesus' statements in the Bible He actually said and which they think were made up. Other leaders confuse faith with financial success. Some argue over days and seasons so that there is no opportunity to speak the Gospel. And the doctrine of eternal salvation has become a matter of personal preference. Some parts of the Church have proclaimed the Gospel in such familiar worldly terms that it becomes a message of psychological self-help. No wonder outsiders do not think Christianity has any more value than society.

The cults have stepped boldly into the void created by the absence of sound biblical teaching. For example, astrology puts the meaning of life into a large, universal setting. Personal and universal meanings blend into one system of thought as ancient as the world and as modern as the sciences. This "new age" combines ancient mystery with new understandings.

Some cults contentedly deal with the meaning of life on lower levels. Getting a person through the day (whether one has any sense of purpose at all) is the minimal intent of cults with a heavy emphasis on meditation or yoga. Many people gladly settle for rising above the daily struggle of life. They hardly worry about purpose; just to survive is enough. But the Church cannot ignore this search for meaning even when people reduce it to "mere survival." Cults are clear signs that the Church must take this inquiry seriously.

THE NEED FOR PERSONAL INVOLVEMENT

People often seek meaning in life through social activity. If one can find a "crusade" of some sort, it seems to give reason for life. Humans generally need to feel that they are involved in their community.

Of course, stressing personal involvement in society is a part of the long tradition in the Church also. Such involvement results from the commitments made in Christian community. What begins there in Baptism, worship, study, and fellowship becomes "alive" in the world. The Christian faith hopes and intends to "become public" in its involvement with the neighbor. The Church offers a level of action grounded in God, who is loved in and through our service to our neighbor as well as on His own.

Cults stress involvement of a different sort. They call for a commitment of intense involvement in that close-knit community within which they reinforce and deepen their cult's tenets. It is almost impossible to be a marginal member of a cultic community. One must be immersed in the common life of the cult. Sometimes this involvement will be liturgical and ritualistic in form, such as in Hare Krishna. Sometimes it will be in the name of social welfare, as in the Black Muslims. At other times it may center around a strong family emphasis, as with the Mormons. With others it may be a "save the world" activity, as one sees in the Jehovah's Witnesses. The point is, the "involving" activity of a cult is not demanded for the sake of outsiders but for maintaining one's own membership in the cult.

Such involvement affords security. It means being needed and wanted. And who does not need security or a sense of being needed and wanted? This is all very attractive and gives a great sense of fulfillment and satisfaction. This sense is vital to implanting, rooting, and maintaining the allegiance of the cult member.

The need to be involved embodies, as noted, a common human need. The Church must also recognize this as a

The cults "suck people in" with an involvement that maintains the closeness of their community through a tight, inner allegiance. In contrast, the Church "pushes people out" into the marketplace as an involving presence of God in the world.

deep-seated *religious* need. As mentioned above, the Church's call to faith is also a call to life. In the Church, God comes to give gifts to His people so that they may give to the world. Therefore, Church certainly has an "inner involvement" that gathers its people to receive God's gifts and for mutual encouragement. But this "inner involvement" ties those who gather to those outside the Church. They are the ones to whom God sends His people as a representation of the divine involvement *in the world.*

THE APPEAL OF THE CULTS IN THIS CONTEXT

The previous paragraphs demonstrate how various needs in today's cultural and religious life provide built-in doors through which the cults enter. Not all cults zero in on or fulfill the same needs, but the proliferation of cults indicates that many people feel that the cults respond to their needs.

30 The appeal of the cults is explained by the fact that cult members by and large feel satisfied that these groups

meet their needs. Some observers charge that cult members are held against their will (and some may indeed be). Others charge that cults brainwash members (and some undoubtedly are). For the most part, however, those who join cults feel they have found a secure place in life. They sense a meaning to which they can attach themselves. They are content. It is important to note this because sometimes we are tempted to insinuate that a member of a cult is not really happy. To approach cult members thus is counterproductive. They joined the cult precisely *because* certain needs have been met. Many find satisfaction in their associations with the cult. To accuse them otherwise will only be a "turn-off."

It is equally inadvisable to point out the "irrational" nature of cults. The authority system to which they subscribe, often supported by "special revelation," will make arguments against irrationality meaningless. They will meet such an assault on their system with the assertion that outsiders cannot possibly understand what the cult stands for or believes. Their rationality can be known and seen only by them.

By the same token any appeal to the ambiguities of life compared to cultic certainties will get a person nowhere. The cult member finds great appeal in the certainties presented within the cult about what is right and wrong. While this idealistic certainty of things appears to be "out of touch" to the outsider, calling attention to it only results in a rebuff.

In like fashion, one gains nothing by questioning the visionary future projected by many cults. The considerable interest in the future manifested in today's world provides fertile ground for cultic imagination. "Far-out ideas" concerning the future get hearings they would not have received in another age. Questions about the future fascinate us. So when cults project a future born of a mix of strange ingredients (but no stranger than many other mixes), they become credible. People whose insecurity causes them to hope for the world to be "fixed" are vulnerable to such visions and promises.

Concern for the future has a firm hold on Christians too. Christ's return stands as a fundamental cornerstone in shaping and forming Christian faith and life. It promises the end of all the old and run-down things of this world as well as the creation of a new heaven and a new earth. We get a sense of direction by knowing where we are going.

A variety of sects within Christendom have taken this fundamental teaching, attached it to a "fulfilled prophecy mode," and projected all kinds of things in heaven and on earth. Predictions of many sorts have captured the imagination of large portions of both the Church and the world. The future is big business today. The cults, with new revelations and new projections, move strongly into this field. They tell people what to believe and how to organize life in light of the "imminent demise of the world and the rise of a new age." Practices like New Age channeling and the teachings of Scientology thrive in this atmosphere.

As you consider how to respond to a cult or cult member, you need to remember that when members of the cults feel persecuted, they are the more convinced of their unity. The bond they feel with the cult intensifies when the cult is under assault. In a type of reverse logic, being attacked becomes proof positive that the forces of evil are trying to overturn the forces of good. Why else would anyone try to condemn "the truth"?

That somewhat twisted logic stands behind some cult members' persistence in approaching outsiders for donations and/or to disseminate "literature"—even to the point of becoming nuisances. Every attempt to discourage them seems only to strengthen their determination and their

33

conviction. Attempts at fending them off serve to affirm the unity of their cause.

IN SUMMARY

The above analyses have only touched the surface of the many factors that encourage people to join a cult. Yet they do offer clues that will help us gain a better point of entry into discussion with those who live in the cults and to speak God's Word faithfully and effectively.

3 UNDERSTANDING THE CULTS

THE DEVELOPMENT OF CULTS

The origins and history of the cults help explain some of the things we encounter in them. The better we understand them, the more likely we can communicate with those involved in them. Keep in mind that, as with any generalities, there are always exceptions.

The cults have generally sprung up around powerful and overwhelming personalities. They rarely are grassroots, popular movements. Without Mary Baker Eddy, Christian Science would not exist. Jehovah's Witnesses owe their existence to Charles Taze

"Our basic premise is quite simple: we believe, after ten years in the field of cult apologetics, that people start and join cults because they have personal needs that aren't being met in traditional churches" (Robert and Gretchen Passantino, *Answers to the Cultist at Your Door* [Eugene, OR: Harvest House, 1981], 13).

Russell. Elizabeth Clare Prophet and David Koresh were sources of personality cults in the nineties.

In addition, for a cult to survive its founder's death, the founder must inevitably leave behind some authoritative writings. Such writings also need interpretation by authority figures, for the average cult member has little to say about the direction of the cult. Cults are virtually always maintained "from the top down."

Second, the cults are almost always a heresy of some mainstream and orthodox religious expression. If you want to understand a cult, you need to understand the source from which it sprang. The personal history of the founding authoritative figure is also important. For example, not many know that Joseph Smith had been a Freemason who was removed from the Masonic Lodge. That helps explain some of the ritualistic structures of Mormonism. Why does the Unification Church seem so Christian as well as pro democracy? Its founder, Sun Myung Moon, has a Christian background in the Presbyterian Church in Korea, from which he drifted into Pentecostalism and anti-Communist activities. Similarly, knowledge of the history of Christian thought reveals the origins of many of the aberrations in today's cults. For example, acquaintance with the development of millennial thought throughout Christian history explains some cultic versions of the approaching end of the world.

There is little new under the sun. Many cults simply rehearse heresies condemned long ago. Of course, to understand a heresy one must also know what the original orthodoxy is. An understanding of Hinduism helps understand Hare Krishna. Knowing something of both Islamic and Eastern religious thought helps to understand Baha'is.

The closeness of these ongoing cultic communities almost always centers on the now-deceased founders. Although they may have had few initial followers and relatively little success in their own lifetime, they did collect a small, close-knit, highly committed group around them. Since many cults die upon the death of their leader, those that survive must have something built into the fabric of their life together to sustain the community. That "something" often is the authoritative writings of the

> Cults begin with authority figures from whom authoritarian teachings originate, usually in written form. These writings, in turn, require authoritative interpreters to promulgate them through changing circumstances and times.

leader. In this way the new leadership can maintain the crucial teachings through the following years. Followers gather to study such remaining documents faithfully. In fact, followers often bestow a messianic character upon the leader after his/her death if it was not claimed before death. This gives a centering place for worship and adoration either to the founder or to the founder's representative in this messianic role.

An authority structure also is needed as a cult's new way of living develops. Someone must interpret writings, supervise life together, and maintain the community as the founder had intended. The community cannot sustain itself with an "anything goes" attitude. With some cults, the inner structure is quite rigid; with others, it is a bit more moderate. It must always, however, develop an inner discipline to hold the community together in a close-knit way.

This inner structure maintains a sense of closeness and "orthodoxy" and helps the fellowship clarify any seemingly obscure truth. If the cult survives many years, new interpretations of the founders' teachings will be needed. A rather rigid authoritarianism and set mode of transferring authority must then emerge. Thus, the cult makes provisions for continuing the original message with any necessary modifications to accommodate the message to new situations. An "orthodox belief system" becomes established. Patterns of life become regimented. A system of initiating new members into the cult develops.

In this way members eventually make commitments more to a rigidly established set of teachings and lifestyles than to the originating authority figure. Yet these developments and interpretations retain their point of reference in the original founder and his/her writings. Such developments may lead on occasion to division and separation within the group. The Reorganized Church of Jesus Christ of Latter-day Saints is an example. It separated from the Salt Lake City community of Mormons over teachings that Mormon leaders developed after the death of Joseph Smith.

The development of "orthodoxy," calling for more and more detailed formulations of doctrine, becomes deeply encrusted with meanings unique to the cult. This, in turn, becomes the origin of the double-talk we mentioned previously. This refinement of the cultic position, perhaps already begun by the founder, leads to an increasingly unique usage of words and ideas. By this time the cult may be on its way to becoming a new world religion— as seems to be the case with the Latter-day Saints and Jehovah's Witnesses.

ENCOUNTERING THE CULTS

It should be obvious by now that responding to cults in a meaningful way requires more than a passing word or two. In order to respond, one must have a decent knowledge of a cult's history, beginning with its founder and continuing through the stages described above to its present state. When one encounters a cult, it is usually well on its way to becoming a full-blown movement. Some may be maturing to the point of becoming new religions.

The developed rigidity of belief and life pattern makes dialogue difficult. One must be prepared for hard work and much frustration coupled with immense patience.

Rigidity of belief, an alternate and sometimes strange lifestyle, and an unwillingness to engage in conversation while pressing their understandings upon their hearers are what one frequently encounters when confronted by members of cults.

This is not to say it is impossible. However, one dare never expect the task to be simple. This rigidity is vital to the existence of cults. Any crack in their belief system can cause the whole structure to come tumbling down. Therefore, there is no room for doubt or question. People in a cult sense this intuitively, even though they may never have consciously thought it out. Therefore, they will not permit the opportunity for anyone to crack the certainty of their system with all its interlocking parts. Their truth is to be proclaimed, not discussed.

"Listening" by cult members merely constitutes a form of politeness. They may be quiet as you explain your point of view, but quietness is not the same as true listening. They will hear only such things as they can answer with their certainty. Given the floor again, they usually proceed as though you had said nothing. Conversations become monologues that you may interrupt on occasion, but they merely tolerate such interruptions until the cult members can resume dispensing their truth to you.

The dedication and commitment found among cult members is impressive. Their task is all consuming, their faith is untouched by doubts or uncertainties, and they are highly knowledgeable about their beliefs. To be sure, their commitment rests solidly in the authority system of their cult. Yet they will often appeal to an authority you recognize, frequently the Bible. For example, Jehovah's Witnesses rarely appeal to the authority of Charles Taze Russell, their founder. They would rather have you reading the Bible in their own translation. They will use words and ideas with which you are familiar. Soon the effect of the

41

double-talk will start taking its toll if you are not careful. The familiarity gives way to confusion. A terrible feeling of uncertainty about your own beliefs may set in. As a result, they have prepared the soil to be sown with the foreign seed of their cultic system.

A way of life accompanies cultic teaching. One must respond to that also. A long string of regulations encompasses the whole of the cultic life. These regulations often seem absurd and unintelligible to the casual observer. To the cult member, however, they are both explainable and integral to their truth. Part of their witness is the lifestyle itself. You cannot respond to one without the other.

The lifestyle emphasis confuses many hearers, for it seems out of touch with ordinary reality. One shies away from getting caught up in such a foreign way of life. The hearer is inclined to label the cult member as weird. That, however, only closes the door to dialogue. Therefore, the Christian must exhibit much patience and a willingness to tolerate (if not understand) such behavior. It does no good to isolate cult members by rejecting their lifestyle out of hand.

This is not to say that understanding and patience will open possibilities for dialogue. When cult members "go public," they seek to recruit new members, not to discuss ideas or lifestyle. If they appear on your doorstep, they have come to convince you. If they stop you on the street, they are not interested in conversation. They want to convert you. It is of great importance to them that they keep separate from the world even when they enter it. They rarely, therefore, try to hide their strangeness. Rather, they use it as part of their witness, as well as a defense against the world that wants to change them.

This becomes a vicious cycle. The more deeply involved they become in the cult, the more they shun the world. And the more they shun the enslaving world "out there," the deeper they withdraw into the cult. They become so enmeshed in their own version of reality that an outsider has great difficulty communicating with them.

The ordinary person, however, seldom encounters cult members in day-to-day living. One only sees them in their evangelistic forays into the world. So, most people identify members of the cults primarily in terms of their proselytizing zeal and little else.

The importance of such missionary activity should not be underestimated. Although the proselytizing member sincerely wants to spread the cult's "truth," other factors also come into play.

43

Many cults require such activity to maintain membership. The two-year service of young Mormon men, for example, is a training period for the whole of life. "Being out on the front line" also serves as a form of protection for the member. Questions and doubts can come when a person has time for reflection. When one is busily dispensing the "truth," one does not have time to reflect on truth. In fact, the more you repeat those "truths," the more likely they will become an integral part of your being.

As a secondary advantage, required proselytizing maintains high involvement and commitment. The life of the cult depends on the involved life of its members. And it gives a sense of personal value, value to other cult members, and to the authorities. A weakening of evangelistic fervor on the part of one member weakens the entire cult. Therefore, all members support and encourage one another in this effort.

This combination of proofs powerfully affirms that the cult member belongs to the group. Such public witness provides evidence of the commitment to a commonly held cause. Self-worth is confirmed, dedication to the cause is proved, and one's place in the community is established.

44   Most people would think cults quaint but harmless if they were content to live and teach in private communes away

from the world. The combination of factors described above, which leads to such a public presence, stirs many people to irritation and opposition. For the Church to address the cults in any significant way, it must take them as they are. It must understand them as best it can and meet them on the ground of their own self-understandings.

When the Church encounters the cults, it must also have its own self-understandings clear. It must give its own witness out of a deep and heartfelt faith of its own in the context just described. To be clear on what that means, we now turn to our own self-understandings and how we might approach the cults with the message of Jesus Christ.

4 TEST THE CULTS WITH THE MARKS OF THE CHURCH

RESEMBLANCES BETWEEN THE CULTS AND THE CHURCH

When members of the Church encounter the cults, some disturbing things will be noted. For example, the Church looks as strange to the world as cults look to the Church. Sometimes the world cannot even see clearly the difference between the Church and cults. You may have observed by now that there are many similarities between the characteristics of cults and their development and that of the Christian Church—a fact we must recognize.

Consider the following in light of what we have written earlier about cults and cultic origins:

There was no grassroots movement in Judaism that became known as Christianity. Instead, there was Jesus. His life and teaching became the authoritative center of what we now know as Christianity. It is not hard to see why the Church was originally considered a cult of Judaism. Christianity focused on one man at significant odds with the religious authorities.

Nor is it hard to understand that the religious authorities were trying to protect the faithful from deviant teachings. If, because of the unusual circumstances, that required crucifixion, so be it.

The Romans, in turn, accepted the Jewish judgment on the matter. They had no way of judging the issue on the basis of religion. But when Rome was burning and they needed a scapegoat to bear the brunt of the anger, they blamed the Christian cult. Christians were expendable, for nobody cared what happened to them one way or the other. So Rome, acting on convenient rumors, outlawed the cult and began to exterminate Christians.

Such oppressive harassment drove the Church underground. Considered illegal by Rome and a cult by the Jews, the believers developed a close-knit, inner life of their own. They withdrew from the world in secret meetings and local communities. However, a liturgy began forming that gave universality to their local gatherings. They soon had tentacles all over the Empire. Nobody gained entry into their inner circle save baptized members. Accordingly, the public knew little about their main teachings, and rumors began to abound concerning what terrible things they did in their meetings. Therefore persecutions multiplied.

It was from this secrecy of their withdrawn life together that Christians emerged to give a witness so powerful that it drew all manner of people into "the Way," as Christianity was first known. Persecutions seemed only to fuel the movement and increase the commitment and inner discipline of the Christians. They became known as those "who have turned the world upside down" (Acts 17:6). The more they were hunted down, the stronger their movement became. Eventually their efforts undermined the very stability of Rome.

Writings appeared that told about this Jesus and His teachings. The members of His close inner circle took up positions of authority, interpreting His life and teachings in both spoken and written word. "Orthodox" understandings began to emerge about this Jesus of Nazareth. The Church gathered the normative set of writings that form the foundations of all teachings concerning this man.

The parallels between this story and the development of cults in our day are obvious. The stress on perceiving, understanding, and thinking rightly in the cults has its counterpart in the orthodoxy of the Church. Both need orthodoxy to recognize heresy.

> Both the Jewish and Roman authorities viewed the Early Church as a cult. It showed many of the marks that we have been using to identify the cults of today.

Nor should the cultic emphasis repulse us. The Christian call to a firm commitment in faith and life touches us in our deepest parts. We encounter a very familiar understanding at this point in the cults.

Even the cults' evangelistic fervor understandably echoes our own commitment to take the Gospel into all the world. Read the Book of Acts for a lesson in evangelistic fervor. We may disagree with tactics, but Christians do not find the fervor strange. It drove the early Christians and has driven many Christians since. When people are convinced they have truth, they also perceive the need to proclaim it from the roofs. Christians and cult members agree on that.

So, a shadow haunts the Church when it confronts the cults. It can be disturbing to recognize something of our own history in their existence.

QUESTIONS RAISED IN LIGHT OF CHURCH AND CULT SIMILARITIES

As we have noted, the Christian Church itself was once considered a cult of Judaism. Islam was once viewed as a cult that combined Jewish and Christian "unorthodoxies." Buddhism was originally considered a cult of Hinduism. When these cults began, who could have said that they would one day become major world religions, recognized in their own right?

Some cults today show remarkable staying power of the same sort. Their growth at times surpasses many Christian denominations. At what point must we stop calling them cults and recognize them as other major religious expres-

How should we respond to the cults? Are we to ignore them? Fight them? Convert them? The unwillingness of cult members to dialogue makes the question difficult and the answer even more difficult.

sions? How dare we judge them? Is not any judgment premature?

In short, many wonder about the position of the Church regarding cults. Since cult members show no interest in dialogue, should we ignore them and hope they go away? Or should we actively seek to stamp out cults by persecuting cult members as "enemies of the truth"? Should we aggressively seek to convert them to Christianity? We need to deal with these questions in order to guide those who are troubled by them.

In order to gain a necessary perspective for dealing with these questions, we must now review some central marks of the Church itself. Here we will see not only crossovers and similarities but also distinguishing and unique features of the Church.

THE DISTINGUISHING CHARACTERISTICS OF THE CHURCH

Two significant characteristics of the Christian Church are a correct use of Scripture and the proper administration of the Sacraments. Simple though the statement sounds, it has profound implications.

For example, Christians accept Holy Scripture as the only authority for what the Church believes and teaches. Many cults, however, agree with that statement, which puts Christians at a loss for words. If both agree on the

51

authority of Scripture, how can they each defend a truth that opposes the other? Or does the cult merely interpret the Scripture in a legitimately different way? No—and the reason why becomes obvious after searching a bit further.

Most cults operate with a "key" to interpretation, a basic writing that forms the authority for understanding the Bible. So, for example, in Christian Science, in Mormonism, and among the Jehovah's Witnesses, Scripture does not stand on its own. Their key to interpretation supersedes Scripture.

At the same time, not all cults speak in the same way of Scripture as an authority. Some accept Scripture only if their own mistranslation is used. Others choose only certain parts of Scripture as authoritative. Of course, non-Christian cults make no such claim at all about the Bible's authority.

The question of scriptural authority, however, is only part of the issue. Methods and principles used in interpreting Scripture distinguish the Church from cults. True, uncertainty and dispute about the meaning of certain parts of the Bible have existed for two thousand years. That is why different Christian denominations exist. There is nothing new or cultic about this kind of an argument.

However, what is generally agreed upon when speaking of the right use of Scripture as a mark of the Church is this: The writings of the Bible belong to the whole Church. Scripture is not and should never be understood or taught in a purely private way. An individual, merely on the strength of his or her own authority, cannot say, "This is what the Scripture says." Even in churches where strong personalities have dominated,

A person who can quote a thousand Bible passages is not necessarily knowledgeable about the truth God reveals in Scripture. Broad themes and motifs interweave throughout the Scriptures. Appropriate use of the Bible must take many things into account. Throwing Bible passages around loosely does not constitute good biblical interpretation.

the word of one person is not sufficient to establish the meaning of Scripture. One voice may have strong influence, but other voices moderate it so that the Church as a whole supports an interpretation. Scripture belongs to the whole Church and needs the balance available through the common understanding of many Christians. Scriptural understanding needs the vertical dimension of the voices of history, as well as the horizontal dimension of today's voices in the Body of Christ for proper interpretation.

In order to clearly proclaim the historically accepted teachings of the Christian faith, the Church has developed creedal statements. For example, the Apostles' Creed sets forth the fundamental truths by which the Church lives. Individual interpretations cannot supersede such statements and remain Christian.

Here we find significant cultic deviations. The authoritative leader typically sets forth new or different understandings. The larger understandings of the Church are ignored, and an individual interpreter becomes the primary source of truth.

It is not always easy to evaluate whether a teaching or group corresponds to the creeds of the whole Christian Church. Every denomination has struggled with this question. Groups within the Christian fold often come perilously close to becoming cults on these very grounds. Thus, we need to evaluate their creeds and public confessions. The private, personal, and often false interpretations of cultic figures will nearly always show themselves most brazenly at this point.

Another dimension relates to the way the Bible is used. The entirety of Scripture forms the authoritative revelation of God. The use of proof passages can be helpful, and many churches certainly use them. But there are some built-in dangers when one resorts to using passages in this way. It gives the impression that the answers to life's questions are found in a variety of short little passages spread all over the Bible.

When a cult member comes with a large number of such "proof passages," it confuses a Christian instructed in this way. The cult member seems to know the Bible far better than the Christian. Rarely does the hearer have even a small number of passages at his/her disposal to respond to this huge array of proof passages thrown out helter-skelter to convince the hearer of the biblical foundations of the cult.

Good and valid though proof passages may be, their usage can never replace nor contradict the larger biblical witness. To isolate certain themes and teachings that the cult chooses to emphasize, without setting them all into their larger context, is not a proper use of Scripture. When cults use passages in this way, the listener must be on guard. Cults selectively choose what they use out of the biblical literature.

Alongside the proper use of Scripture, the Church also has considered the proper administration of the Sacraments as one of its distinguishing characteristics. The Sacraments, of course, intimately tie to the Word.

55

There they gain their meaning and efficacy. The two go together.

"But as for you, continue in what you have learned and have firmly believed, knowing from whom you learned it and how from childhood you have been acquainted with the sacred writings, which are able to make you wise for salvation through faith in Christ Jesus" (2 Timothy 3:14–15).

Most cults, though, attach little importance to what we call the Sacraments. These groups may develop some rituals that have some sort of sacramental meaning, but rarely do the biblical sacraments stand at the heart of their life together. Here one can usually make very clear distinctions, for Baptism and Holy Communion are typically at the heart of life in the Christian Church, while they are at best marginal in most cults.

So, for example, consider the Mormon "baptism for the dead" ritual. In Scripture, the Sacraments (as well as the rites of the Old Testament) strengthen the faith of believers for living daily life. This is a basic foundation of the Word itself. By contrast, the Mormon "baptism for the dead" has nothing to offer the living in their struggle to live the faith.

If we are to be faithful witnesses to Christ in our encounters with the cults, we must know the substance of our own faith. Members of the cults, with both their commitment and their knowledge, often bewilder Christians. Faithful commitment to and a sound understanding of the Scriptures are absolute necessities for standing against the cults. They are even more necessary if Christians set out to address people in a cult with the intention of calling them to the way of Jesus Christ.

5 WHAT WE CAN LEARN FROM THE CULTS

At this point you may be thinking that a Christian response to cult members seems futile. That would underestimate the power of the Holy Spirit. We ought to prepare ourselves and seek opportunities where the Spirit can do what we cannot do on our own.

With preparation, we discern what Christians look like from another perspective. Our study can help us discover the needs of our world and what the Church should do in this modern world. It can help us evaluate the image we project in today's world. In short, this "look through the back door" of our lives may help us to become more faithful servants of our Lord. Because the cults fill part of this world to which we are called, any insights we gain can also open the doors to encountering the cults with Christ.

A REFLECTION WORTH REFLECTING UPON

How winsomely do we present the Gospel? Does our witness issue from a life filled with meaning and joy, or do we speak out of a sourpuss necessity? Do we speak and live "with gentleness and respect" (1 Peter 3:15), so that people recognize the presence of Christ in us? Are our evangelism efforts clearly the work of concerned and caring people, or merely an attempt to swell our numbers? Does our lifestyle reflect our words? As we watch and reflect on the way members of the cults make their witness, we are called in turn to reflect on how our own witness is being made and heard.

LESSONS FROM THE CULTS

A Lesson about Authority

Lesson number one relates to the nature and place of authority. What is proper use of authority? The Scripture is our authority for teaching and life. The Church proclaims an authoritative message. Our life is governed by authorities in the home, in the Church, and in society. Authority is necessary to maintain order. Freedom can exist only within the context of an ordered authority.

The Church must reflect on how to testify to an authoritative Word and how to exercise its own authority without imposing it. How can the Church model the authority of Christ that He exercised in a servant mode? How can we also observe the space for freedom that comes with the rule of Christ? These major challenges arise as the Church orders its life in contrast to the cults.

"Moses said to the Lord, 'Oh, my Lord, I am not eloquent, either in the past or since You have spoken to Your servant, but I am slow of speech and of tongue.'
"Then the Lord said to him, 'Who has made man's mouth? Who makes him mute, or deaf, or seeing, or blind? Is it not I, the Lord? Now therefore go, and I will be with your mouth and teach you what you shall speak' " (Exodus 4:10–12).

About the Nature of Doubt and Questioning

The absolute confidence that they know truth is a striking feature of cult members. However, this raises a question: "Who could possibly believe so confidently that they have no serious doubt?" Such certainty often appears to be a front and a fraud. At the same time, we Christians seldom express our own doubts or questions when telling others about the certainty of our salvation in Jesus Christ.

In light of this, we may pause for reflection about the place of questions and doubts in the midst of great faith. It is hardly appropriate to laud doubt or to encourage questions as though there were merit in this. Yet doubt inevitably attacks our faith. We live in a world where sin surrounds us. The evil one is at work. Doubt always lies close at hand.

Harsh winds blow through our lives regularly. We must reflect on what we see, hear, and feel. Although not always easy, faith must directly confront the realities of life. The strength of faith lies in its object, the cross of Christ, and is measured by how well it bends with assaults and still stands tall. Faith can be imagined as a tree bowing but not breaking before strong winds, not by a hard, brittle, unbending pane of glass that is smashed by the wind.

We do not give our best witness, therefore, by hiding our doubts, but by telling how our faith is sustained in the face of our doubts. We do not boast about our questions, but we can acknowledge them while speaking of the confidence God has raised up in us through Jesus Christ. Our witness shines forth most brightly when we boldly give it in the face of so many uncertainties. Our faith does not refuse to recognize problems connected with believing. Rather, faith lives even while we recognize all the problems.

The holy writers were willing to express boldly such doubts and questions. In so doing they "tested" their faith against God, as it were. His gracious Spirit won them to faith in the face of their questions. Read the Psalms. Listen to the prophets tell of the struggles they endured when God called them to their tasks. Let Job speak of his doubts in the midst of his faithfulness. The testimony of Scripture shows the truth of this. However, we must add, this differs greatly from "tempting God." To place one's self deliberately in the path of unbelief and then to challenge God is quite another thing. That misuses what God has given us and is very different from expressing doubt.

Doubts and questions are our human voices talking. In the midst of those voices, another voice rings out and calls us to believe. It directs us to the suffering, death, and resurrection of Jesus Christ and calls us to trust Him. That voice does not quiet all questions and doubts, but it is the one sure word we have and can speak in the midst of our questions and doubts. That voice, the message of life, assures us that God's supreme love holds the earth in

His embrace. It calls us to come into God's gracious presence with confidence. We cast our doubts and questions onto God and leave them with Him while we worship and adore Him, love and serve Him, tell others of His grace, and live in reverence before Him. That is Christian witness.

About Commitment and Dedication

We cannot deny that the cults can teach us much about commitment and dedication. But a negative lesson needs to be learned first: Our commitment must not be to a pastor, a denomination, or a cause. That is the message cults send out. They reach out in order to draw people into a community centered on an authoritarian figure.

The positive lesson is that our commitment remains first and always to the God who has revealed Himself in Jesus Christ. Christ's living presence resides within His Body, the Church, the Christian community. Therefore, we invite people to come into the living presence of Christ in that community.

The commitment and dedication of cult members provides another lesson for us. Christ calls us to confess our faith in both word and deed. Christianity is a way of life born of our faith. Our witness is all of one fabric, with

63

words and lives knit together as one piece of cloth. That is our witness to Christ. Christian witness is not an either/or; it is a both/and. Words without deeds or deeds without words—neither is a complete witness. Both must be blended into one life, one person, and one witness.

About Sound Biblical Study and Knowledge

The cults insist on strong educational programs to insure the knowledge and commitment of their members. So also, each of us needs to spend more personal time with God's Word. But the cult's success presents a clarion call to the Church to upgrade its educational programs.

We need far more than a proof-text knowledge of the Bible. Knowledge in how to use and interpret Scripture as a whole must be provided. Until members of the Church willingly engage in a serious study of this sort, the cults will find ready ears in the very backyard of the Church itself. Members of the Church have every right and responsibility to insist on this from those who have been prepared to teach and preach in the Church.

About the Place of Doctrine in the Church

Just as we need to know the Bible better, so we also need to understand how everything the Bible says fits together. That's what we call "doctrine." Christian doctrine sets

64

forth in an orderly way what the Church understands in regard to such things as who Jesus is, how God saves us and brings us to faith, how He cares for our faith through Word and Sacrament, what will happen at the end of the world, and so on. Those who teach Christian doctrine attempt to show both how individual doctrines fit into the whole of Scripture and also how biblical teaching answers contemporary questions.

The continued wrestling with how to present these teachings is a sign that Scripture's unchanging truth must always connect with life's changing circumstances. Were it not such a constant struggle to present old truths in new settings, we could simply reprint the writings the Church prepared in the second, fifteenth, or nineteenth centuries. However, every age calls for a new application of Christian faith and life. Thus, the study of Scripture in the light of the present situation of people is important. It helps connect Scripture and our age.

Cult teachings, on the other hand, are rigid; they cannot be shaped for life in the world. They are splendid examples of teachings formulated without serious contact with the world they intend to address. The hearer has a hard time understanding what is so important about them. They just hang like isolated statements, suspended above life as we experience it. Why bother with them?

This does not say that biblical truth changes to meet the whims of the world. In fact, it often contradicts "the wisdom of the world." However, the way in which doctrine states the truth must always speak to the changing condition of the world. It is the never-ending task of the Church to connect the truth of Scripture to everyday life, and it is the task of the Christian to search out and study the one truth of the Gospel that sets us free.

"Let brotherly love continue. Do not neglect to show hospitality to strangers, for thereby some have entertained angels unawares" (Hebrews 13:1–2).

About the Sense of Community

Loneliness abounds in our culture. Humans need a place where they have a sense of belonging. Cults use the trump card of providing a strong, well-knit supporting community. A huge part of their attraction has to do with the way they reach out to lonely people and promise them a place where they will feel warm and accepted. For this reason, cult members frequent public places where people feel lost or friendless. Their appeal is to offer these people a place of care.

The Church is intended to be such a place. One of the most important words in the Church's evangelistic vocabulary is the word *hospitality*. That is a very significant biblical word. Even a casual reading of the New Testament reveals the expectation that the Church will provide a caring, loving, accepting, encouraging, and supporting community. It was a primary characteristic of the Church in the Book of Acts. The New Testament letters present such expectation as a central understanding of how Christians live together.

The Church of today has much to learn from the cults in this regard. Where the face of the Church turns to the lonely and the needy, drawing them up into her arms of care and compassion, there the Body of Christ shows itself. The more inclusive the Bride of Christ becomes in her practice of hospitality, the more she shall reveal the presence of Christ in her midst.

Such a community makes sense to those whom the cults now reach with great success. The lesson for the Church is relatively simple to express in words: Be the caring body you are created to be. It is, however, very hard to enact, for being hospitable means opening arms and lives to people with whom we may not be comfortable. The Church should not be afraid to learn this lesson from the cults. Many surprises await the people of God where the Church's openness to the stranger reflects Christ's reaching out to the world in love.

About Experience Coupled with Knowledge

From time to time the Church needs to be reminded that it has no reason to fear "experiencing the faith." The strong emphasis on "knowing" Scripture at times overshadows the human need for emotional expression. "Knowing God" is not necessarily the same thing as "knowing the Scriptures." To "know God" includes much more than mere head knowledge. It has to do with the relationship that God initiated in our Baptism. To "know Scripture" is to understand its content and be caught up in the sweep of its power. Both are important, but sometimes the Church stresses understanding too much and underplays the possibility of experiencing the presence of God.

The Church may learn something from the interesting blend of knowing and experiencing that the cults have created. There is a mystery about life that defies knowing. It calls for experiencing life. Through drama, poetry, music, art, ritual activities, and other related ways, one can become swept up into the power and delight of the presence of "the otherness" about life beyond our sight. The Church dare not neglect this form of knowing God. Its

68

stresses encountering God in the Scriptures and through the Sacraments, but does not preclude the use of experiences such as those mentioned. In short, the Church must reclaim some of the mixture of mystery and knowledge that comprises its faith.

EVANGELISM IN THE SHADOW OF THE CULTS

Apathy surrounds us on every side. It is hard to find a person strongly committed to anything consequential. While the cult members' zeal and enthusiasm almost look refreshing in this context, that same exaggerated zeal and enthusiasm repel many. Cult members are guiltier of "bad taste" in many cases rather than outright rudeness. Yet they have a reputation for running roughshod over the feelings of those they encounter.

> "Oh give thanks to the Lord; call upon His name; make known His deeds among the peoples! Sing to Him, sing praises to Him; tell of all His wondrous works" (Psalm 105:1–2).

Once more there is a lesson for the Church to learn. On the one hand, Christian people have every reason to have zeal and enthusiasm. They have been called in their Baptism to the fullness of life in Christ. What greater gift can they have? The lack of enthusiasm and zeal, which seems to characterize much Christian evangelism, causes our Christian witness to fall flat. People wonder why we aren't more enthusiastic and dedicated if the Christian faith is so great. Where is the infectious vibrancy that should characterize one who carries the word of life?

Perhaps some of this dullness comes from a fear of being confused with cultic types of witnessing. Perhaps we take too much of an edge off our fervor and devotion lest we offend the other person. Surely we can take a warning against using bad taste in approaching others. Surely we do well to recognize that there are appropriate times and places for the sharing of the Gospel. However, none of this excuses us for dampening the joy and power of the Gospel. Christian witness need not be obnoxious, pushy, or irritably aggressive. It can be winsome without being wearisome, forthright without being forbidding, bold without being boorish.

In short, we must not let a negative image of witnessing to the faith give us reason to shut down our witness. We cannot escape our responsibility for witnessing. We can, however, learn to do it with good taste and in consideration of others.

6 CHRISTIAN WITNESS TO THOSE IN CULTS

In 1 Peter 3:15 Christians are encouraged to engage unbelievers "with gentleness and respect." Cult members often tempt us to respond to them with rudeness because we perceive them to be rude. We tend to be impatient with them because they show little civility toward us as they press their message on us. But Peter reminds us that every person is important to God, even rude, obnoxious, and inconsiderate people. So, we must deal with cult members at their worst as well as at their best with all "gentleness and respect."

"Gentleness and respect" dictate some don'ts, as well as some things to do. We will begin with the things to avoid and then speak of the positive possibilities for Christian witness.

SOME DON'TS

1. *Don't be hostile.* Although many cults may consider you their enemy, you are not part of a Christian "defense system." Cult members are not enemies to be conquered. They are fellow humans who need Christ. Witness to Jesus, who calls us to deal "with gentleness and respect."

2. *Don't slam the door in their face.* This does not mean you cannot be firm with them. With "gentleness and respect," you can explain that your schedule prevents a visit just now. Or an appointment can be made for a more convenient time. This will give you opportunity to learn something about them from other sources and will also allow time to prepare what you want to say to them. It establishes a ground for such conversation as is possible with them. You may also set time limitations within which the exchange can take place. However, slamming the door in their face without respect gives no witness to them and is not in keeping with "gentleness and respect."

3. *Don't argue heatedly.* Logic will not prevail. Cults work with a revelation and authority foreign to what you will recognize. Heated arguments do not give witness to cult members. This tactic only confirms them in their

error. Such arguments do not lend themselves well to "gentleness and respect."

4. *Don't show anxiety.* If you have done your homework and are comfortable with your own faith, you need not worry about making a fool of yourself. You can ask intelligent questions and make intelligent responses. Anxiety encourages them to press their case. It does not raise sympathy for you. Be calm and cool in your own witness "with gentleness and respect."

"Do not be anxious about how you should defend yourself or what you should say, for the Holy Spirit will teach you in that very hour what you ought to say" (Luke 12:11–12).

5. *Don't rely on yourself alone.* Pray for the Spirit in rich measure. God has promised to stand by you to give you strength and wisdom from above. The Spirit will lead and guide you. Remember: lack of success is not a sign of an absence of the Spirit. You can rely on the divine promise. With this promise firmly in hand, you can speak "with gentleness and respect."

Having stated these negatives, the positives can be set forth under two headings: "Be Patient" and "Be Loving."

BE PATIENT

This is a difficult counsel to keep in light of hectic schedules and the premium we place on time. Yet it is part of the "gentleness and respect" to which Peter calls us.

Now that you know some of the human and spiritual needs that drive people to a cult, you might be more likely to see cult members as other than merely strange and weird. When we see others as hurting souls in need of Christ, we are more inclined to be patient.

Their commitment need not cause us to be curt. We can respect them for being people of commitment, even though we consider their commitment a destructive one.

"Settle it therefore in your minds not to meditate beforehand how to answer, for I will give you a mouth and wisdom, which none of your adversaries will be able to withstand or contradict" (Luke 21:14–15).

We can even appreciate their commitment to an authority figure or to authorized sets of writings. Christians, committed to Christ and the Scriptures, testify of Him. Understanding such things may contribute a bit to having patience. In the same way, their zealous evangelism is understandable to us. We can honor and respect it, for we, too, zealously proclaim our message to the world.

In short, our patience can be helpful in granting them integrity in their own right. To wrong them by disrespecting them is not an appropriate response, even if they have been rude or have wronged us.

BE LOVING

Christian "gentleness and respect" requires also that we be genuinely and warmly concerned for cult members. They are not mere statistics that would look good on our church roster. Nor are they merely "things" to be manipulated by pulling the proper strings and quoting appropriate Bible passages to them. (Remember, this is a major objection to their approach.)

Cult members as sinful humans need Christ just as we do. Our Christian concern has to do with their total welfare. As a good rule of thumb, treat them as you would want them to treat you.

There will certainly be disagreement—and even anger—with them on occasion. Jesus, too, disagreed with many and got angry on occasion. But these people with whom we disagree are creatures from the hand of the same Lord who is the Father of us all. They are people with needs common to all other humans. They, too, are people for whom Jesus died. When we see them through the eyes of God, who gave His Son into death for the world, they won't look the same to us. Nor will we act the same. Discussions and contacts with those blinded by cultic error will take place in truth, with patience and love. Hate, spite, and malice will have no place in these conversations. The loving hand of Christ will reach out to them through us. And we will speak and act under the direction of the Holy Spirit.

The prophet Isaiah promised, "For as the rain and the snow come down from heaven and do not return there but water the earth, making it bring forth and sprout, giving seed to the sower and bread to the eater, so shall My word be that goes out from My mouth; it shall not return to Me empty, but it shall accomplish that which I purpose, and shall succeed in the thing for which I sent it" (Isaiah 55:10–11). Lay hold of that promise.

RESOURCES

Breese, Dave. *Know the Marks of Cults*. Wheaton: Victor Books, 1975 (revised 1986).

Enroth, Ronald M. *The Lure of the Cults*. Chappaqua, NY: Christian Herald Books, 1979.

Herbert, Kern. *How to Response to Jehovah's Witnesses*. Rev. ed. St. Louis: Concordia, 2010.

Kaiser, Edgar P. *How to Respond to the Mormons*. Rev. ed. St. Louis: Concordia, 2010.

Lochhaas, Philip H. *How to Respond to the New Age Movement*. Rev. ed. St. Louis: Concordia, 2010.

Martin, Walter. *The Kingdom of the Cults*. Minneapolis: Bethany House, 1965 (revised and updated with Ravi Zacharias, 2003).

Mather, George A., Larry A. Nichols, and Alvin J. Schmidt. *Dictionary of Cults, Sects, and World Religion*. Grand Rapids: Zondervan, 2005.

Passantino, Robert, and Gretchen Passantino. *Answers to the Cultist at Your Door*. Eugene, OR: Harvest House, 1981.

Starkes, M. Thomas. *Confronting Popular Cults*. Nashville: Broadman Press, 1972.

Van Baalen, Jan Karel. *Chaos of the Cults*. 4th rev. ed. Grand Rapids: Eerdmans, 1962.

WEB SITES

www.lcms.org—The Commission on Theology and Church Relations has some short pamphlets that give the basic facts about various cults.

etext.lib.virginia.edu/nrms/—The Religious Movements Web site was begun by Prof. Jeffrey K. Hadden and merely sought to compile as much information as possible. Since the death of Prof. Hadden in 2003, the site has been archived, but the archives are available for public usage.

NOTES

CHAPTER ONE

1. David Breese, *Know the Marks of Cults* (Wheaton, IL: Victor Books, 1975), 16.

2. Ronald Enroth, *The Lure of the Cults* (Chappaqua, NY: Christian Herald Books, 1979), 20–21.

3. Walter Martin, *The Kingdom of the Cults* (Minneapolis, MN: Bethany House, 1979), 11.

4. Jan Karel Van Baalen, *Chaos of the Cults*, 4th ed., rev. (Grand Rapids: Eerdmans, 1962), 14, quoted in Martin, *Kingdom of the Cults*, 14.

Notes